To Susan 19·77
from Mrs mr Sparkes

Horse and Pony Quiz Book

John Bullock
Illustrated by Gwen Green

Hamlyn
London • New York • Sydney • Toronto

Published 1975 by
The Hamlyn Publishing Group Limited
London • New York • Sydney • Toronto
Astronaut House, Hounslow Road, Feltham,
Middlesex, England.
© Copyright 1975 The Hamlyn Publishing Group Limited
ISBN 0 600 34467 3
Printed by Litografía A. Romero, S. A.
Tenerife (Spain). D. L. TF. 466 - 1975

Contents

Page

Questions

Stabling and Grazing	10
Watering and Feeding	12
Grooming	14
Saddlery	16
Care of the Horse or Pony	18
Horsemanship	20
Hunting	22
General Knowledge	24

Answers

Stabling and Grazing	28
Watering and Feeding	32
Grooming	36
Saddlery	39
Care of the Horse or Pony	44
Horsemanship	51
Hunting	56
General Knowledge	59

Questions

Stabling and Grazing

Novice Questions

1. What are the main advantages and disadvantages of keeping a pony at grass?
2. Why is it wrong to keep a pony on rich grass in the spring?
3. If a pony is kept at grass, what rules should be observed?
4. What additional food should a pony kept at grass be given, and when?
5. Name three of the best types of fencing available for a field used for ponies.
6. Why are loose boxes better for ponies than stalls?
7. Why are stable doors divided into two parts?
8. Why are narrow doors bad?
9. Why should doors open outwards?
10. What is the best sort of latch for a stable door?
11. Why is barbed wire fencing bad for horses?
12. Name three types of straw used for bedding.

Intermediate Questions

13. Why are ponies often healthier when kept at grass?
14. What does it usually mean if a pony starts to rub in late winter when his coat is thick?
15. How should drainage be arranged in a well constructed box?
16. Why are central covered drains in the floor considered to be bad?
17. What do you know about the need for ventilation?
18. Are mangers necessary?

19. How should a manger be fixed?
20. How high should a hay rack, or hay net, be?
21. Where should a bucket be placed in a stable?
22. What are the three best types of buckets for stable use?
23. Name plants, trees or shrubs which are dangerous for ponies to eat.
24. Why is barley straw not considered to be good straw for bedding?

Advanced Questions

25. What is stained land?
26. Straw is commonly considered the best form of bedding material. Name four others.
27. Give three reasons for putting a horse or pony on sawdust or wood shavings.
28. Why is trussed or bundled straw better than baled straw for bedding?
29. What are the essential points to watch if sawdust or wood shavings are used?
30. In a stable what would you do about windows and light fittings?
31. How would you keep a manure heap?
32. Name three important items of equipment when mucking out a pony kept on wood shavings or sawdust.
33. Which rug would you use for a pony kept out, and how does it differ from other rugs?
34. Name the four most common rugs and sheets used for a stable-kept horse or pony.
35. What is the difference between a surcingle and a roller?
36. How should a rug be put on a horse?

Surcingle

Roller

Watering and Feeding

Oats

Novice Questions

37. The digestive system of a horse has three essential requirements if it is to perform its work properly. What are they?
38. What is the first rule of good feeding?
39. Why should a stabled horse or pony be given plenty of bulk food like hay?
40. How should any change in the feeding routine be made?
41. Why should you always water before feeding?
42. Is it wrong to keep water continuously in the stable?
43. Why are oats good for a horse?
44. Why should care be taken when feeding oats to ponies?
45. Why are horse and pony cubes popular?
46. Why is chaff or bran often fed with horse and pony nuts?
47. How long should new hay be kept before being fed?
48. Why is a bran mash of special value to a sick pony or one which is suddenly prevented from working?

Intermediate Questions

49. What are the typical carbohydrate foods of the horse?
50. What are proteins?
51. Name six of the ingredients which usually go into the making of horse and pony cubes.
52. How many main types of hay are usually fed to horses, and what are they?
53. Which is the best feed: a soft or hard hay?
54. Which of the following can sometimes be substituted for hay: wheat straw, oat

straw or barley straw?

55. Why does a bath make a bad water trough?
56. If a stabled pony does not have constant water in his box, how often must he be watered?
57. What should you do if a pony takes a full draught of water when it is hot and sweating?
58. Is it harmful for a pony to drink from an ice-covered trough?
59. What is the best way of watering?
60. Why is clean fresh water important?

Advanced Questions

61. Approximately how much does the stomach of a pony hold?
62. How long will a pony usually graze before stopping to rest?
63. Why do muscles need sugars?
64. How would you tell a good meadow hay?
65. Why is clover hay not as good as sainfoin?
66. Why are lawn mower cuttings dangerous if fed to horses or ponies?
67. What should be done to a pasture with surplus grass in the early summer if it is required for grazing ponies?
68. When feeding mashes, what are the three main points to remember?
69. In what form should oats be fed?
70. What is 'fibre', and how many kinds are there?
71. Why is fibre important in feeding?
72. How frequently should a horse's teeth be checked?

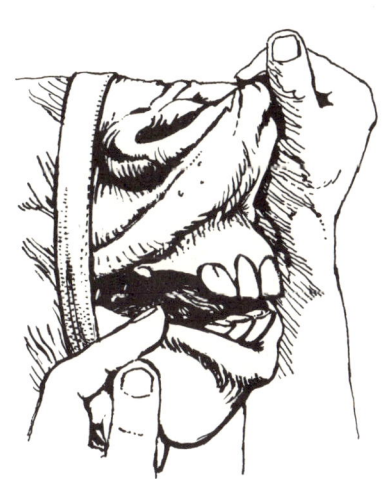

Grooming

Novice Questions

73. What are the five main objects of grooming a horse or pony?
74. What is the instrument for cleaning out a horse's hoof called?
75. (1) How many brushes are there in the usual grooming kit?
    (2) Can you name them?
76. What is a wisp, and what is it used for?
77. What is a stable rubber used for?
78. What is the difference between pulling and hogging a mane?
79. Why is it undesirable to pull the tail of a pony living out at grass?
80. What is required for tail pulling?
81. Name the four principle types of clip.
82. What is the best type of clip for a pony out at grass?
83. Why is the hair left on the legs on a hunter clip?
84. Name the reasons for plaiting a mane.

Intermediate Questions

85. Why should the hoof pick be used working downwards from the heel towards the toe?
86. What should you do after cleaning out the hoof?
87. Should a dandy brush be used on the mane and tail?
88. Where should a wisp not be used?
89. What is strapping?
90. When is it best to groom?

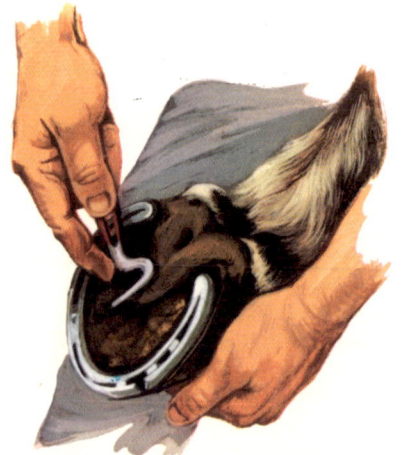

91. How long should a wisp rope be before being woven?
92. What are the main reasons for clipping a horse or pony?
93. When are the first and last clips of the season usually made?
94. How many plaits should a mane have?
95. How should a tail be cut square?
96. How frequently should a hogged mane be clipped?

Advanced Questions

97. How do you prevent water from becoming lodged in the hollow of the heel when washing the feet?
98. How should a mane be 'layed'?
99. Why is hoof oil necessary?
100. In a hunter clip care must be taken to ensure that the saddle patch is correct. What effect would a saddle patch cut too far forward have on the horse's looks?
101. Where should you start when clipping a fretful horse?
102. What is a bang tail?
103. How do you pull a switch tail?
104. What are 'cat hairs'?
105. What material is a tail bandage made from?
106. Should a tail bandage be left on a horse at night?
107. Why is it wrong to wet a tail bandage?
108. How should the long hairs which grow in the jowl regions and at the back of the tendons be removed?

Square cut tail

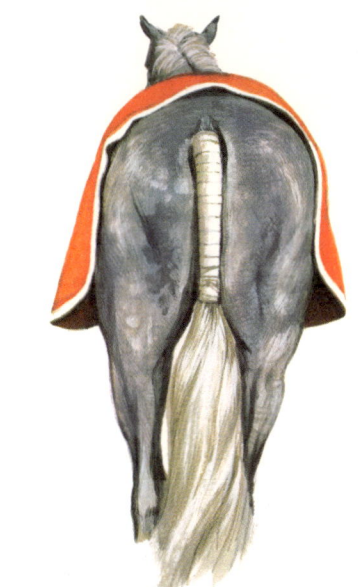

Tail bandage

Hunter clip

Saddlery

Snaffle bridle

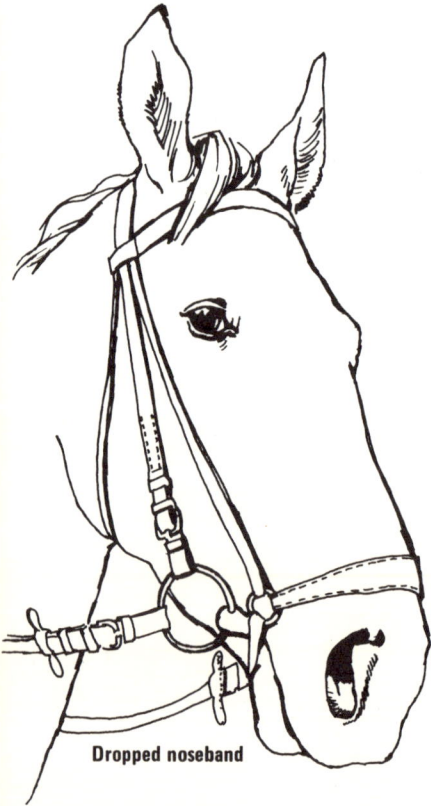

Dropped noseband

Novice Questions

109. In stable talk what is saddlery usually called?
110. Which of these oils is good for leather: castor oil, dubbin, linseed oil, mineral oil, neatsfoot oil, glycerine?
111. What is the difference between a full panel saddle and a half panel saddle?
112. Name the three kinds of saddle linings, and give their advantages and disadvantages.
113. How should a saddle be carried?
114. If a pad saddle is fitted with D's instead of stirrup bars, what sort of stirrups should be used?
115. What is a numnah and why is it used?
116. Name the four main materials that girths are made from and say which is best.
117. Name the parts of a snaffle bridle.
118. What is the difference between a bridoon and weymouth and where are they found together?
119. What is the purpose of a breast plate and crupper?
120. What is the purpose of a standing martingale?

Intermediate Questions

121. Why are steel stirrup irons better than plated metal or nickel?
122. What is a saddle tree? What material is usually used in its manufacture?
123. On most stirrup bars there is a hinge that allows the point to be turned up. What is the reason for these points, and should they be up or down when a horse or pony is being ridden?
124. How do you measure the size of a saddle?

125. How would you measure the width of a horse or a pony when fitting a saddle?
126. If you had to make a wither pad quickly what would you use?
127. The neck strap buckle of a martingale should be on which side of the neck?
128. How much of a numnah should be visible when a horse is saddled?
129. Why should you always allow the horse or pony to ease the bit out of his mouth slowly when you are taking off the bridle?
130. What are the differences between a standing martingale, a running martingale, and an Irish martingale? What are their uses?
131. Should a curb chain be made of a series of linked metal rings, leather or elastic?
132. What is the difference between a Pelham and a Kimblewick?

Advanced Questions

133. What is approximately the difference in girth length from buckle to buckle for a small pony and a very large hunter?
134. Name the three leather girths.
135. How should a dropped noseband be adjusted?
136. In a double bridle should the bridoon be above or below the bit?
137. When should a curb chain come into action?
138. What are the differences between a 'flash' noseband, a 'grakle' noseband and a 'Kineton' noseband?
139. What is a 'brush pricker'?
140. How is a snaffle bit measured?
141. Where would you find a Magenis, a Scorrier, a Fillis, a Dick Christian, or a French Bradoon?
142. What is the chief cause of the deterioration in leather saddlery?
143. What is a bib martingale and why is it used?
144. When would you use a Hackamore?

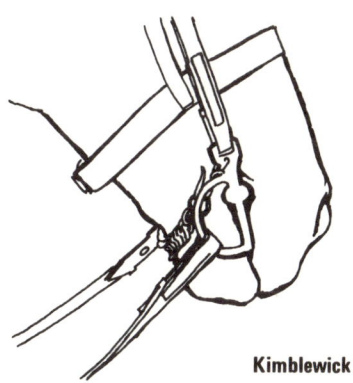

Kimblewick

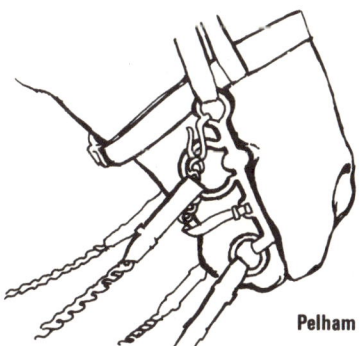

Pelham

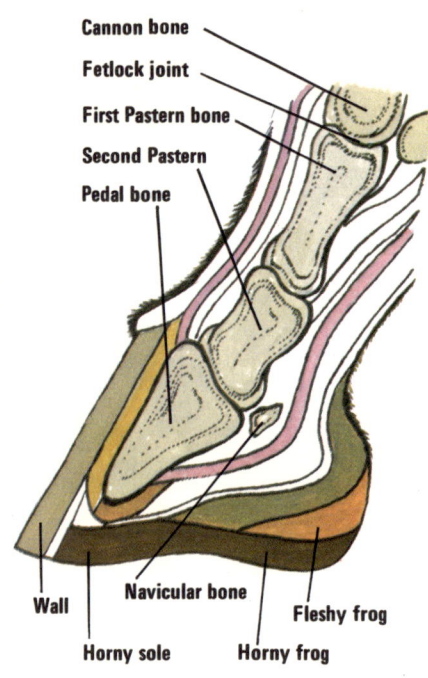

Care of the Horse or Pony

Novice Questions

145. Name the three main external sections of the foot and explain the parts they play.
146. Explain the two systems of shoeing.
147. Name four tools usually used by a farrier.
148. What is a 'clench'?
149. What is usually the difference in shape of a fore shoe and a hind shoe?
150. What are roaring and whistling?
151. What are a 'good doer', a 'bad doer' and a 'dainty feeder'?
152. What is an 'over-reach' and how should it be dealt with?
153. What are ringbones, sidebones, windgalls and splints?
154. What is thrush, how is it caused and how should it be dealt with?
155. What are girth galls, and what would you do if your horse was suffering from them?
156. What are the three most usual ways of administering medicine?

Intermediate Questions

157. What shape should the sole of a horse's foot be if it is in a healthy state?
158. What makes up the interior of the foot?
159. Name the six definite stages of hot shoeing.
160. If a pony is lame, how would you find out which leg was causing the trouble?
161. What are the main causes of laminitis or 'fever of the feet'?
162. What is colic and how would you deal with it?
163. What are the frequent causes of colic?
164. What is the normal body temperature

of a horse or pony?

165. How would you tell if a horse has a cold in the head?

166. What is 'strangles' and what are the symptoms?

167. What is meant by 'broken wind'?

168. Describe and name the four most common types of wounds to which ponies are susceptible, and say how they are usually caused.

Feather-edged shoe

Advanced Questions

169. Explain the difference between 'fine nailing' and 'coarse nailing'.

170. Why can coarse nailing be dangerous?

171. What is a 'feather-edged shoe' and why is it used?

172. How would you tell which part of a leg was affected if a horse was lame?

173. How would you tell if a horse or pony has laminitis and how would you deal with the trouble?

174. If a horse is uneasy and restless, is off his feed, and keeps on looking round at his flanks, kicks at his belly, and frequently gets up and down and rolls, what would you expect the cause to be?

175. How would you treat a horse with a cold in the head?

176. Describe the cough of a broken winded horse.

177. What is 'azoturia'?

178. What is consumption in a horse, and at what age is it more likely to appear?

179. How would you protect a horse against lockjaw? How is it caused and what are the symptoms?

180. How would you give a horse a drench?

Horsemanship

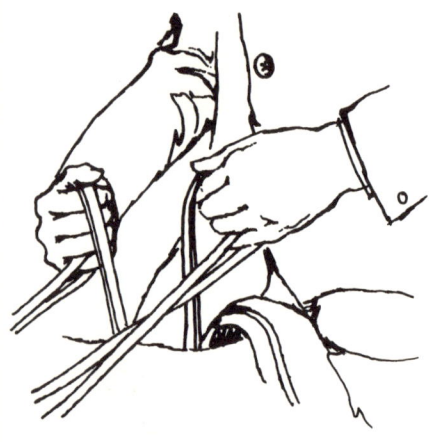

Novice Questions

181. What is the first thing to do before mounting?
182. Why is it wrong when dismounting to throw a leg over the horse's withers?
183. Is it correct to mount and dismount on the nearside or the offside of a horse?
184. What is meant when people refer to 'the seat'?
185. How would you measure whether the stirrup leathers were of the correct length?
186. What is the difference in pace between the trot and the canter?
187. How should you hold the reins of a double bridle in both hands?
188. The word 'aids' has two meanings. What are they?
189. What is meant by natural and artificial aids?
190. When riding how should you carry a whip?
191. How would you increase a horse's pace to a walk or a trot?
192. How would you decrease the pace or halt?

Intermediate Questions

193. What are the objects of dressage?
194. What is meant by 'shoulder in'?
195. What is meant if a horse is said to be cantering 'true' or 'united'?
196. Give the four main reasons why a horse pulls.
197. Should you increase or decrease the severity of the bit on an excitable or pulling horse?

198. Describe the two alternative positions for riding at the gallop.
199. What is the action of the hands and the legs when they are used as aids?
200. How can the voice be used as an aid?
201. What happens when a horse approaches a jump?
202. Describe what happens as a horse takes off, goes over the jump, and lands.
203. Why is it wrong when schooling to keep on jumping fences in a continuous straight line?
204. How would you find out which is a horse's stiff side and which was his soft side?

Advanced Questions

205. When is a horse said to be cantering 'false' or 'counter-lead'?
206. What is meant by a dry mouth?
207. Why should a horse try and swallow its tongue or try and put it over the bit?
208. What is a 'half pass'?
209. What is a turn on the forehand?
210. What is known as rhythm in dressage?
211. When is a horse said to be 'on the bit'?
212. Define the term 'loose rein'.
213. How many steps to a stride are there to the pace of a walk, trot, canter and gallop?
214. What would you do if a horse developed the habit of rushing his fences?
215. When schooling a young horse to jump would you prefer to increase the height or spread of the jump?
216. Why is a well-placed ground line useful in schooling a horse to jump?

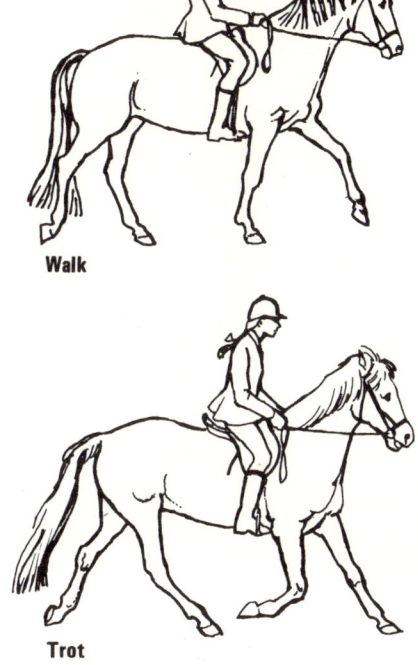
Walk

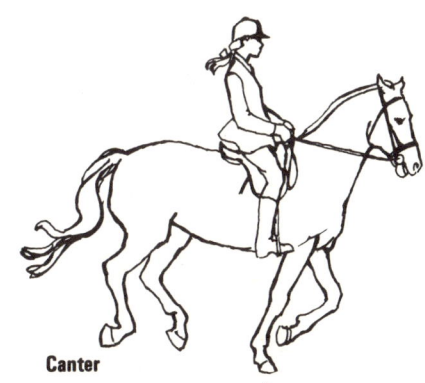
Trot

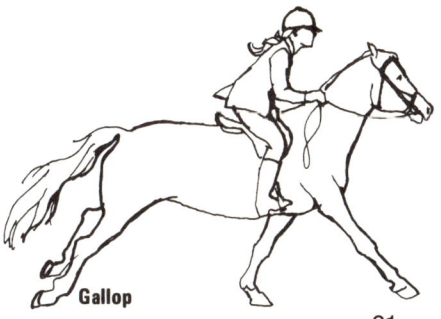
Canter

Gallop

Puppy walker

Hunting

Novice Questions

217. When does cub hunting start and end?
218. When is the official end of the fox hunting season?
219. Who are puppy walkers?
220. What are the titles of the Hunt staff?
221. How should you dress for a cub hunting meet?
222. Why is a hunting whip and thong important? How must it never be used?
223. Why should you put one leg forward and hit the saddle flap with your hunting whip when standing by a covert out cub hunting?
224. What does the term 'riot' mean out hunting?
225. When would you be allowed to get in front of hounds?
226. What is the shortened form of 'beware' used at hunting?
227. How are hounds counted, or how do you 'make a pack'?
228. What is the term 'Holloa-Away'?

Intermediate Questions

229. Name six of the different types of food which can be given to hounds to keep them healthy.
230. Why are cubbing meets held early in the morning?
231. What is usually considered to be the correct dress for the Hunt staff on hound exercise?
232. Why are hounds given plenty of roadwork during exercise?
233. How should you refer to a fox?
234. What is the Hunt button?
235. When is the term 'Hounds please!' used?

236. What is a hunting tie or stock?
237. What is known as 'the country'?
238. When are hounds said to be 'at fault'?
239. What is meant by 'running up together'?
240. When are hounds said to 'draw up wind'?

Advanced Questions

241. What is the difference between a Hunt button worn with a scarlet coat and a black coat?
242. How does the Master wear the tails or feathers of a Hunt cap?
243. What speed is a 'fadge'?
244. What is a 'bona fide hunter'?
245. What is known as a hound hunt?
246. What would it mean if you heard a whipper-in say to the Huntsman 'We want a couple, sir'?
247. What is meant when a pack of hounds is said to be 'carrying a good head'?
248. What is an 'entered hound'?
249. What is meant if a hound 'throws his tongue'?
250. What is a babbler?
251. When is a hound known as 'toe down'?
252. What is meant by 'all on'?

Hounds moving off from a meet

General Knowledge

Fulmer snaffle with cheek pieces

Novice Questions

253. What is an Australian cheeker?
254. How many nails are there in a standard horse shoe?
255. How did a grakle noseband get its name?
256. How did the Kimblewick bit get its name?
257. What is known as conformation?
258. What is a Palomino?
259. What is a draught horse?
260. What is a dragsman?
261. How would you describe a draw rein?
262. What is a dutch slip?
263. What does flecked mean?
264. What is a filly?

Intermediate Questions

265. What is a log?
266. What is the average recommended size for a pony loose box?
267. When is the best time for a mare to foal?
268. What is flagging?
269. In saddlery, what are known as runners?
270. What is horse-sick?
271. What is a Horse Standard?
272. Where do you find a garter?
273. Where is the seat of corn?
274. What is a Connemara?
275. How would you describe a brougham?
276. What are false ribs?

Advanced Questions

277. Who was the first hunting monarch in England?

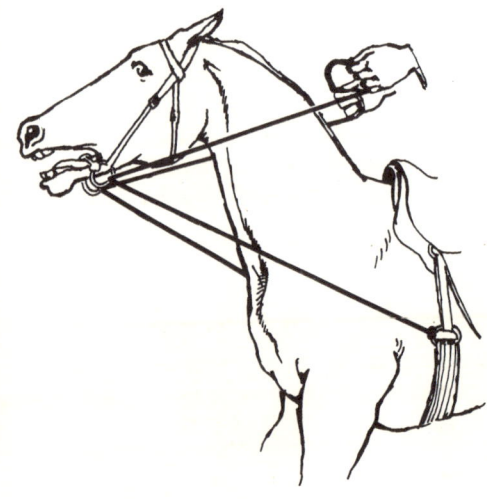

278. What is a hybrid?
279. What are Lonsdale girth straps?
280. What is a loriner?
281. What is a troika?
282. What is a wagon-lock?
283. What is a garron?
284. In a horse's mouth what is known as the 'mark'?
285. What is a jaunting car?
286. Where would you find a jarde or jardon?
287. What is a ewe neck?
288. Beans are the nutritive foodstuff sometimes given in horse's feed. Give another definition of the word beans.

Hybrid

Answers

Stabling and Grazing

Novice Answers

1. The main advantages of keeping a pony at grass are that he is provided with more freedom. He can exercise himself and graze at will. He can roll at will and get more fresh air.

   The disadvantages of keeping a pony at grass are the wind and cold of winter and the flies of summer. Ponies can also be difficult to catch, especially in summer. Mud cakes the coat in winter, and an unclipped pony can sweat up more easily.

2. There is a chance that the pony will get too fat and may develop fever of the feet known as laminitis. The main symptoms are heat in the feet and a reluctance to to walk. The pony tries to get the weight off his front feet and, in so doing, stands on his heels with feet forward.

3. The pony must be seen each day. A constant supply of fresh water is essential and the pony's feet must have regular attention. In winter extra feed will be necessary, and he will require worming at regular intervals throughout the year.

4. A pony at grass will require extra food in winter before he starts to lose condition. A thin or 'poor' pony has little protection against cold, wind and rain. Good quality hay should be fed early and pony nuts or quantities of oats, bran and beans should be fed.

5. Strong post and rail fencing high enough to discourage a pony from jumping out of the field provides the best form; then comes a thick hedge or, failing that, good posts with tight wire strands. Barbed wire is not recommended.

6. Loose boxes give more comfort and freedom and enable the horse or pony to lie down more easily.

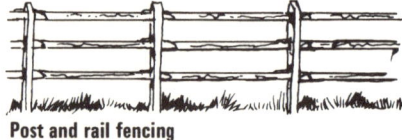
Post and rail fencing

Posts with tight wire strands

Hedge

7. So that the top half can be left open to provide additional ventilation, and so that he can see out.

8. Narrow doors can cause injury to the horse, particularly in the hip area, and saddlery can also be damaged if the horse brushes against the door posts.

9. To save disturbing the bedding every time the door is opened, and to provide easy access to the box if the horse becomes cast.

10. A safety latch that prevents the horse opening the door, either by pushing or using his teeth. It must be of a type that will not catch the horse or its saddlery.

11. A horse or pony may well get tangled up in barbed wire and hurt itself, particularly if the wire becomes loose. He can also ruin his mane and tail by rubbing against barbed wire and pulling out and damaging the hairs.

12. Wheat straw, oat straw and barley straw.

Intermediate Answers

13. They get more fresh air and can exercise themselves. However, care must be taken to ensure that they are not allowed to get too fat in summer.

14. The pony may have lice. If so, a good delousing powder should be used.

15. Towards an outside open channel with a very slight slope to the box floor.

16. They are insanitary if not kept clean, can get blocked, and the gratings break more easily.

17. Horses need plenty of fresh air at all times. They are more likely to keep clear of coughs and colds if they have good ventilation in their stables.

18. Not essential — a good feed bowl on the floor is as good, and is nearer to the horse's natural feeding position.

19. The manger should be securely fixed to the wall, and deep enough to stop the horse from throwing its feed out. There should be a broad edge to prevent the

Some plants are dangerous only when eaten in excess

horse from biting or damaging the manger, and it should be installed in a position that prevents the horse from getting cast underneath.

20. The hay rack should not be positioned too high up the wall. If it is too high, the horse will not have a natural feeding position and seeds and dust will get into its eyes.

21. The bucket should be placed near the door in a position where it will not be knocked over and will not easily be overlooked. It must be kept full.

22. Plastic is cheap to replace and light to carry; rubber is noiseless but relatively easy to topple over; metal is noisy and dents easily.

23. Ragwort, meadow saffron, horsetails, green bracken, St. John's wort, ground ivy, hemlock, water dropwort, foxglove, yew, laburnum, rhododendrons, laurel, privet, acacia.

24. Its husks are bad for a horse because they can get stuck in its throat. Combine-harvesters now remove much of the husks, but barley straw is inferior to wheat straw.

Advanced Answers

25. Land fouled with droppings through horses having been kept there too long or on too small an acreage.

26. Sawdust, wood shavings, peatmoss and dried bracken.

27. If the horse eats its bedding; if it is allergic to the dust from the straw; or if there is a shortage of labour because sawdust or wood chippings are quicker to muck out and keep clean.

28. In baled straw most of the fibres are broken or crushed which means that elasticity is lost and drainage is affected.

29. The bed is inclined to heat and rot when it gets wet. The droppings should be removed at regular intervals along with any wet patches of sawdust or shavings where the horse has staled.

30. Windows provide ventilation but they

must be protected by iron bars, and all lights should also be protected or made of specially toughened glass. The switches should be of the safety type.

31. The manure heap should be kept tidy and divided into three sections. One section should be for the old rotted manure ready for the garden, the second section should be in the process of rotting, and the third should be the one in daily use.

32. Wire rake, skip and rubber gloves.

33. The New Zealand rug. It is made of waterproof material to withstand the weather and has leather straps to go round the hind legs to keep the rug in position when the pony rolls.

34. Night rug, day rug, sweat sheet, fly sheet.

35. A surcingle is a 2½ by 3 inch wide piece of web passing over the saddle and secured by a strap or buckle. It is frequently used with racing saddles. It can also be a hemp or jute surcingle sewn onto a rug as a means of keeping it in place.

A roller is made of leather, hemp or webbing and is used with a night or day rug to keep it in place. It is fastened by one or two buckles, and has two padded panels to fit on either side of the spine. There are various patterns including the arch type which eliminates pressure on the horse's spine and prevents him from getting cast.

36. The rug should first be folded in two so that as it is put over the horse's back the front buckle can be fastened first before the rug is folded open and straightened. The roller or surcingle can then be fastened.

Watering and Feeding

Novice Answers

37. (1) Water   (2) Exercise   (3) Bulk Food
38. Feed little and often in order to keep as near as possible to the natural method of feeding.
39. So that the digestive organs are always kept filled, as they are when a horse is grazing.

    Without adequate bulk it is not possible to maintain a successful digestive process.
40. Any adjustments to the type of food or its frequency should be made gradually and spread over several days.
41. So that undigested food is not washed out of the stomach.
42. No. A pony will frequently take a short drink during or after a feed if water is kept in a stable. This will not be harmful because it will not have the same effect as taking a long draught.
43. Oats provide a balanced, nutritive and readily digested food on which horses thrive.
44. Small ponies respond very quickly to a highly concentrated feed such as oats, and they can consequently become unmanageable and difficult to ride.
45. They are easy to feed and store, and are made up of a variety of ingredients which help provide a balanced diet.
46. Feeding an additive such as chaff or bran ensures that the food is masticated properly and there is salivation to moisten the food before swallowing.
47. About six months because new hay can prove to be indigestible.
48. A bran mash has laxative properties. All

stabled horses can benefit from a weekly bran mash.

Intermediate Answers

49. Oats, bran, hay and grass — particularly the coarse fibrous grass which is characteristic of autumn and winter grazing.

50. The so called 'flesh-forming' substances.

51. Oats, bran, maize, locust bean, barley, grass meal, linseed cake, groundnut meal, molasses, vitamins and minerals.

52. Two main types of hay are usually fed to horses. They are meadow hay and seed hay.

53. Hard hay, because soft hay is always of inferior feeding value.

54. Oat straw, which is the straw of spring. Sown oats are palatable because the straw is thinner than straw which has grown through winter. Winter straw has very little nutritive value, however, and only provides bulk.

55. The sharp edges of a bath can injure the knee of a horse or pony.

56. A pony needs watering four times a day in winter, and five or six times a day in summer. Water should always be given first thing in the morning, on return from work, and before feeding.

57. The pony should be walked about after he has drunk.

58. No. There is no harm in a pony drinking from an ice covered trough.

59. If you make sure that water is always available in a stable or field, the pony will drink as and when neccessary.

60. Although ponies will sometimes drink

Four types of hay are:
1 Meadow
2 Timothy
3 Sainfoin
4 Clover mixture

Linseed *(boiled)*

Barley *(boiled)*

Carrots *(sliced)*

Oats *(crushed or bruised)*

Pony nuts

The diet can be supplemented with additional feedstuff

stagnant, smelly and discoloured water, nothing affects a pony's condition as much as dirty and inefficient watering arrangements.

Advanced Answers

61. The stomach of a pony holds about 2-2½ gallons, but its walls are very elastic and will expand to some extent.

62. Some ponies only graze for about three hours before resting, but their habits differ considerably.

63. To enable them to contract and perform work.

64. When meadow hay is hard and crisp to touch, and sweet to smell it is usually referred to as having a good 'nose' to it. It should be greenish to brownish in colour. If it is yellow or dark brown it has deteriorated.

65. Sainfoin is highly nutritious and probably the best of the more common hays. Clover hay, though rich, is very often dusty and susceptible to mould. It is wasteful, too, because it slips easily through a hay rack or net. Well-harvested clover or sainfoin hay should always be golden.

66. Short grass cuttings can choke a horse or pony. This can cause severe colic and diarrhoea, and unless veterinary treatment is given quickly death can result.

67. The easiest plan is to graze a few bullocks with the ponies during the 6-8 week spring 'flush' period. If not, a mowing machine should be used when the grass reaches about 6-8 inches in length to reduce it to about 2 inches long. The cut grass can be left on the pasture to dry and wilt so that it can be eaten later.

68. (1) They must be thoroughly scalded and left covered for at least half an hour before feeding.

    (2) They must not be fed too hot.

    (3) The residue of the mash must be removed from the manger or feed bowl before it becomes fermented, stale or sour, and taints other food.

69. Oats are fed either whole, crushed, rolled or boiled. It does not matter which type is used.

70. Fibre is hard, tough material in hay, straw and the outer husk of oats. It is of two kinds, one of which is digested and one which is not. The digested one is known as cellulose and its derivitives, and the other is ligrin or woody fibre.

71. Both digestible fibre and woody fibre are needed by the horse or pony for efficient digestion. If concentrated foods only are fed without fibre, dilation of the bowel, pain and illness can occur.

72. At least once a year, or if there is any falling off in condition, due to the inability to masticate properly.

Grooming

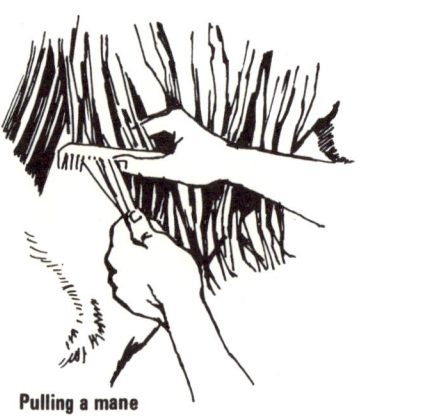

Pulling a mane

A hogged mane

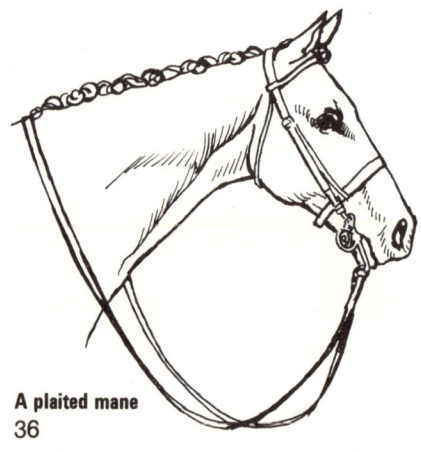

A plaited mane

Novice Answers

73. Grooming:
    (1) promotes health.
    (2) maintains condition
    (3) prevents disease
    (4) ensures cleanliness
    (5) improves appearance

74. A hoof pick.

75. (1) Three
    (2) The dandy brush
    The body brush
    The water brush

76. A wisp is a tightly woven rope of hay and straw used for promoting circulation, and as a means of masssage to develop and harden muscles.

77. A stable rubber gives a final polish after grooming.

78. **Pulling** is done to thin out an over thick mane; to reduce a long mane to the required length; or to permit the mane to lie flat.

    Hogging the mane is the complete removal of the mane with clippers.

79. Pulling the tail of a pony at grass deprives it of natural protection in the dock region.

80. A body brush, a water brush, a mane comb, trimming scissors and a tail bandage.

81. The full clip, the hunter-clip, the blanket-clip and the trace-high clip.

82. The trace-high clip because it is a compromise between partly clipping a pony and not clipping a pony at all.

83. The hair left on the legs acts as a protection against cold, mud, cracked heels and injury from thorns.

84. Plaiting is done for neatness, to show off the neck and crest, and to train the hair to fall to the side desired.

Intermediate Answers

85. To prevent any risk of the hoof pick penetrating the soft parts of the frog.

86. Tap the shoe to see that it is secure, and then run the tips of the fingers round the clenches to see that none are risen.

87. No. It is wrong to use a dandy brush on a mane and tail because it removes and breaks the hairs leaving them thin and unsightly.

88. Wisps should not be used on all bony prominences and the tender loin region.

89. Strapping is the thorough grooming of a horse or pony from start to finish.

90. Grooming can always be carried out more efficiently after a horse has been exercised rather than before, since exercise warms up the skin, loosens and raises the scurf to the surface and opens up the pores.

91. 6 - 8 feet in length.

92. The reasons for clipping are — to enable a horse to carry out fast work without undue distress, and to keep a horse in condition by avoiding heavy sweating. In addition it permits a horse to work longer, faster and better, and facilitates quicker 'drying-off' on return from work; it also saves labour on grooming and prevents disease.

93. The first clip of the season is usually made in October but the last clip should not be delayed later than the last week in January.

94. There should be eight plaits including the forelock, but if more are necessary there should always be an even number including the forelock.

95. The tail should be cut with scissors with the help of an assistant who places his arm beneath the root of the tail. The cut is then square when the tail is carried naturally.

96. About every three weeks.

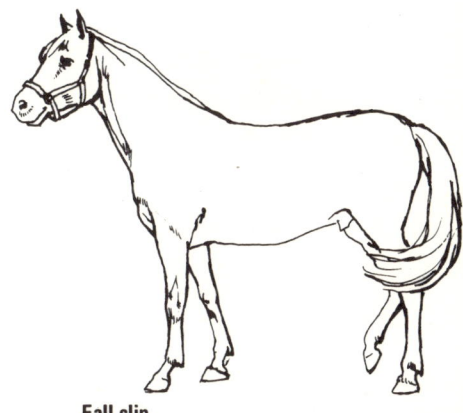
Fall clip

Blanket clip

Trace-high clip

Washing feet

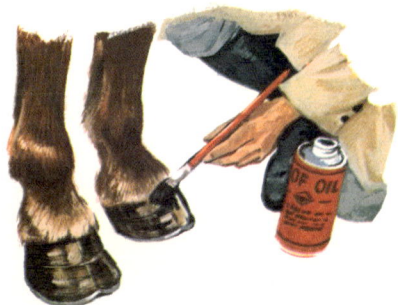
Hoof oil

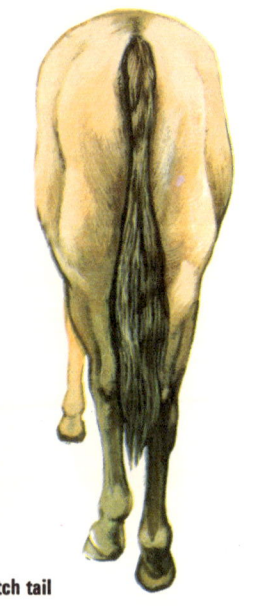
Switch tail

Advanced Answers

97. Use a bucket of water and one end of a water brush when washing the feet. The thumb of the hand holding the foot should be pressed well into the hollow of the heel to keep out the water.

98. Dip the end hairs of the water brush in the bucket of water, shake it out and apply it flat to the mane. The hairs should be brushed from the roots downwards so that they are left slightly damp

99. Hoof oil improves the appearance and is beneficial to broken or brittle feet.

100. The horse will look short in the shoulder and long in the back.

101. It is always as well to start clipping a nervous or fretfull horse at the shoulder region.

102. A bang tail is when the ends have been cut off square at the level of the points of the hocks.

103. A switch tail is pulled to about half the length of the tail, and the ends are allowed to grow in a natural point.

104. Cat hairs are the long hairs which appear in various parts of the coat, giving an untidy appearance to the horse several weeks after it has been clipped.

105. Tail bandages are made of stockinette 2½ - 3 inches wide.

106. No. A tail bandage should be put on after exercise and grooming and removed at evening stables.

107. A wet tail bandage may lead to shrinking of the material and injury to the tail.

108. By plucking with the fingers, a few being removed with each grooming, or with a comb and scissors.

Saddlery

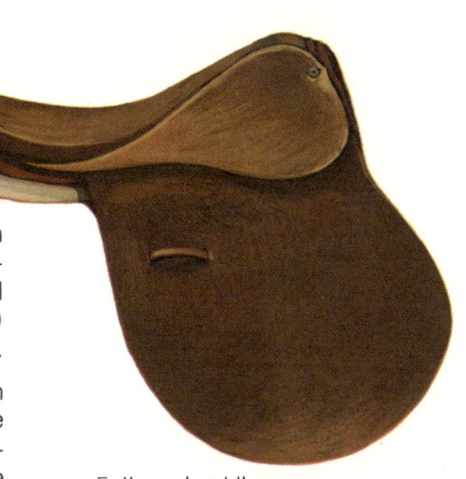

Novice Answers

109. Tack.

110. Vegetable oil and animal oil in the form of castor oil, dubbin, glycerine or neatsfoot are good for leather. Linseed oil or mineral oil (motor oil is an example) become hard and are bad for all leather.

111. A full panel reaches almost to the bottom of the saddle flap, and is lined all the way down. It has only a short sweat-flap, or underflap, between it and the girth tabs.

    A half panel reaches half-way down the saddle flap. It usually has a large sweat-flap reaching almost to the bottom of the saddle flap.

Full panel saddle

112. The three kinds of saddle lining are serge, linen and leather.

    Serge is absorbent, but it is hard to keep clean and does not wear well. Linen wears longer than serge. It is easy to wipe over and keep clean, and it also dries quickly. Linen, however, is not as long lasting as leather if the saddle is kept properly and used frequently.

113. Either with the front arch in the crook of the elbow, allowing the bridle to be carried over the same shoulder, or along the thigh with a hand over the front arch.

114. Safety stirrups, because any device which prevents the stirrup leather from coming off the bar is potentially dangerous.

115. A numnah is made of felt, leather, sorbo rubber, sheepskin or nylon fabric and is cut to the shape of the saddle. It can be used to rectify a badly stuffed or ill-fitting saddle, as protection for the horse's back. In the case of a sore back, a felt numnah can be of help if it is cut to leave a hole over the sore spot.

The correct way to carry a saddle

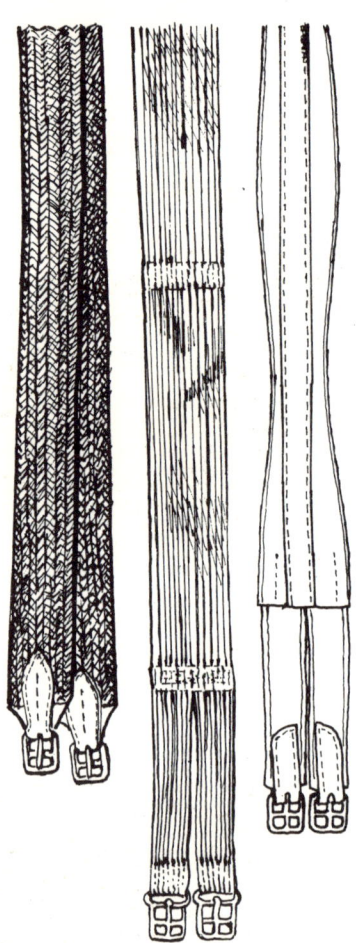

116. The four main materials are web, leather, nylon and string.

    Web girths do not wear well and can sometimes snap without warning, and for this reason a single web girth should never be used.

    Leather girths are good. They are long wearing and if kept supple they should not cause girth galls.

    String girths last well and are easy to clean. They also let the air through and help prevent galling. Nylon girths are similar to string but tend to slip more. They also stretch when new.

117. The parts of a snaffle bridle are the headpiece and throat lash, brow band, two cheek-pieces, nose band, bit and reins.

118. The bridoon is a fairly thin mouthpiece snaffle which can either have ring or eggbutt cheeks and the weymouth is a bar bit with cheeks. Both can be used to form a double bridle.

119. The breast-plate prevents the saddle from slipping back, and the crupper steadies the saddle and prevents it from slipping forward.

120. Prevents the horse from throwing up its head beyond the point of control.

Intermediate Answers

121. The best stirrup irons are made of steel and hand forged stainless steel is the most satisfactory. Plated metal chips and flakes, whereas pure nickel is soft and can bend. It also has a yellow appearance.

122. A saddle tree is the frame on which a saddle is built. It is usually made of beech wood, but many modern saddle trees are now made of laminated wood bonded under pressure and formed in a mould. Other materials are also being tried including fibreglass.

123. The points prevent the stirrup leathers from slipping off when a saddled pony is being led without a rider. The points should never be up when the pony is being ridden.

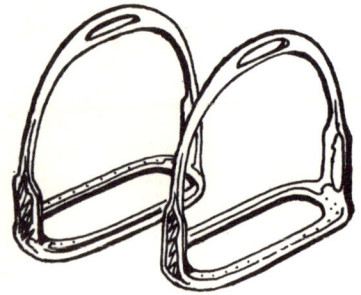

124. From the studs to the side of the pommel to the middle of the cantle.

125. With a length of malleable non-springy material about two feet in length. This should be moulded over the withers about three inches back from the shoulder where the front of the arch of the saddle should rest. When lifted off, the inside shape can be pencilled onto a piece of paper and sent to the saddler.

126. A piece of woolen or cloth material like a stable rubber. It is placed between the pommel of the saddle and the horse's wither where the front arch of the saddle presses down onto it, or is too wide for the horse.

127. The near side.

128. The numnah should be slightly larger than the saddle and visible for about one inch all round the saddle. Before tightening the girths the front of the numnah should be pulled up into the front arch of the saddle.

129. Because he may throw up his head if the bit is dropped out quickly. In doing so, he could also get caught up in the bit and hurt his mouth. If this happens he could become difficult to bridle.

130. The standing martingale is the simplest in action. It is a leather strap with a loop at either end, one of which fastens on to the girth through the forelegs, and the other onto the noseband. There is also a neck strap to keep it in position.

    The running martingale is similar but a little more complex in its action, the reins being passed through the rings of the martingale.

    Spectacles or Irish martingales have no effect in the positioning of the head. The martingale is a short piece of leather with rings at either end through which are passed the reins. Its use is confined to preventing both reins ending up on the same side of a horse's neck.

131. All three are quite permissible but the linked metal ring type is the most common.

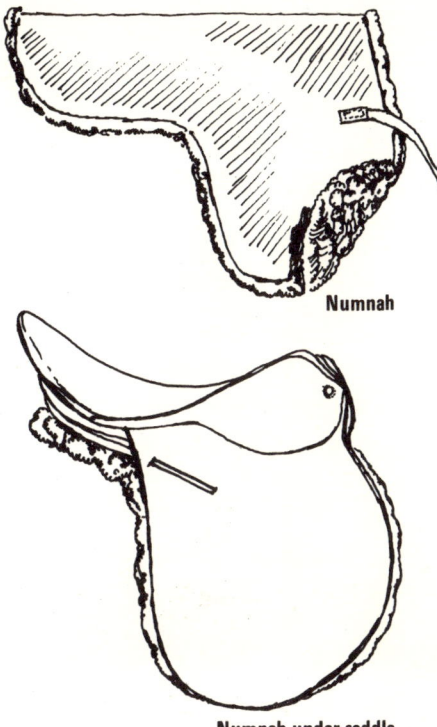

Numnah

Numnah under saddle

Measuring the saddle

Double bit

Grakle noseband

132. The Pelham has all the characteristics of a curb bit, but it is used independently of a bridoon, and has two reins. The Kimblewick is a member of the Pelham group but it has a single rein.

Advanced Answers

133. Girths are usually made in two inch sizes from about 36 inches in length for a small pony up to as much as 54 inches for a very large hunter.

134. The three most common varieties of leather girth are the Balding, Atherstone and three fold girths.

135. The dropped noseband should be carefully fitted so that the front strap is well above the nostrils and the back is in the chin groove. It should be adjusted so that it is tight enough to prevent the horse or pony from crossing his jaw or opening his mouth wide, but not so tight that it prevents the flexing of the jaw.

136. In a double bridle the bridoon should be above the bit.

137. The curb chain should come into action when the cheeks of the bit are drawn back to approximately 45 degrees to the mouth.

138. A flash noseband may be used with a standing martingale. It consists of a strong cavesson noseband with the addition of two crossing straps sewn to the centre of the nosepiece, which are fastened below the bit. The point of pressure on the nose is a little higher than on the usual drop noseband. The grakle noseband has the lower straps fastened under the bit, and the top ones

Magenis

above with a connecting strap at the rear to keep them in place. In recent years the grakle has sometimes been called the figure of eight or 'cross-over' noseband.

The Kineton or Puckle noseband consists of two metal loops with a connecting nose strap which is adjustable at both ends. The centre of the nosepiece is usually reinforced by a leather covered piece of metal, the loops being fitted on the inside of the bit rings and behind the mouthpiece.

Dick Christian

139. A brush pricker is fixed onto the side of a bridle to cause a horse sufficient surprise and discomfort to persuade him to change course. It is used on animals who have one-sided mouths or are stiff in their backs, or who hang to one side or another particularly when racing.

140. Snaffle bits are measured between the rings when laid flat.

141. They are types of snaffle.

142. Loss of fat content in the leather as a result of neglect.

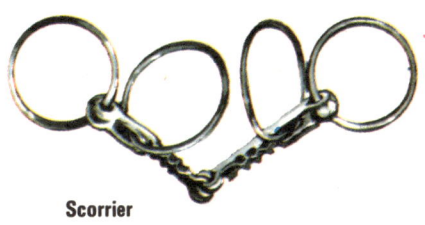

Scorrier

143. A bib martingale is usually used by a racehorse trainer. It is rather like a running martingale but the centre piece of leather between the two branches is a precaution against an excited horse getting caught up or putting his nose between the branches, or straps, holding the rings.

144. A Hackamore is a popular type of bitless bridle useful on a horse whose mouth may be damaged or who will not go well in a normal bridle.

Hackamore

Care of the Horse or Pony

Hot shoeing

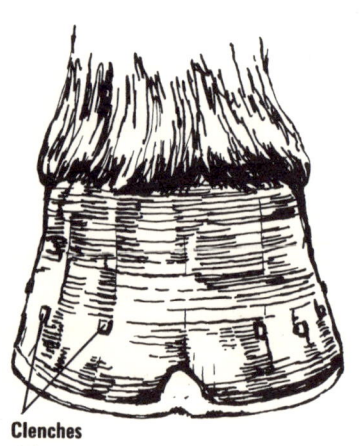

Clenches

Novice Answers

145. The three main sections of the foot are the wall, the sole and the frog.

The wall grows downwards from the coronet and goes right round the foot. At the heels it goes inwards to form the bars of the foot. The coating on the outer surface prevents undue evaporation from the horn and stops it degenerating and becoming brittle.

The sole protects the foot from underneath. It is quite thin and care should be taken to prevent it from being damaged.

The frog is nature's anti-slipping and anti-concussion device in the foot. It makes contact with the ground first and appart from allowing the horse to gain a good foothold, it also takes up the jar of impact with the ground.

146. The two systems of shoeing are 'hot shoeing' and 'cold shoeing'. In hot shoeing the shoe is specially made to fit the foot. It is heated and tried on hot, so that adjustments can be made before it is finally cooled and nailed on.

In cold shoeing the shoe has already been made, and any alterations have to be made when it is cold.

147. The four tools are the hoof parer, clinch cutter, rounding hammer and rasp.

148. A clench is the end of the nail where it penetrates into the wall of the foot, and is then turned over and twisted off leaving a small piece projecting outwards. It is known as a 'risen clench' when the shoe is worn and the small piece of nail projects too far from the hoof.

149. Usually, the fore shoe has only one toe clip, and the hind shoe has two quarter

clips to assist in keeping the shoe in position and giving greater security.

150. Roaring and whistling are abnormal noises made by a horse when travelling at a fast pace. Roaring is an exaggerated form of whistling, and both result from a paralysis of one of the nerves of the throat. An operation is usually necessary, but fortunately the condition is extremely rare in ponies.

151. A good doer is a horse which manages to keep in good condition even when he has to put up with indifferent feeding.

A bad doer is a horse which falls off in condition however carefully he is fed and looked after.

A dainty feeder is one who is usually fastidious in clearing up his feed.

152. Over-reaches are self inflicted wounds of the fore tendons or bulbs of the heels, due to being struck by the toe of the hind foot, usually when a horse is galloping or jumping. The treatment should be the same as for a bruised wound or cut. Examine the hind foot, and make sure that the hind shoes have quarter clips. Over-reach boots should be used in cases where this type of trouble occurs frequently.

153. Ringbones are bony enlargements of the pastern bones either low on the coronet or high above the coronet. The more serious are those which involve a joint. Sidebones form in the heel region so that flexibility of the heel can be lost.

Windgalls are swellings of joint sacs just above and to the sides of the fetlock joint. They are seldom painful or cause lameness when they are first formed, and afterwards they usually give little trouble.

Splints are small bony knobs which form on the splint bone, the cannon bone or both. They are troublesome when forming but later they may cause little inconvenience, unless they involve the knee joint or press on the suspensory ligament. Lameness is rare from this complaint after a horse is six years old.

154. Thrush is a foul condition of the cleft of the frog due usually to neglect. The cleft should be carefully cleaned out daily and dusted with boracic powder or other dry dressings.

155. Girth galls usually appear on the soft skin behind the elbow. They can be caused because the pony is too soft in condition, and the girth has been too tight, too loose or too broad. It is best not to use a saddle for a few days until the skin has hardened, and then make sure a string girth is used. If it is not possible, the girth should be slipped through a clean piece of inner tube from a car tyre. A pad of lambs wool put beneath the girth will also relieve any pressure and pain on the injured spot providing it is kept soft. Frequent applications of salt water, methylated spirit, or witch hazel lotion will help the skin to harden.

156. Medicine is usually administered in the feed, in the water or on the tongue, or by injection.

Intermediate Answers

157. The sole should be rather like a saucer which has been turned upside down, ensuring that it gives a good foothold.

158. The interior of the foot consists of bones, joints and sensitive structures, which are all liable to injury if the wall, sole or frog becomes damaged.

159. The six stages are removal, preparation, forging, fitting, nailing on and finishing.

160. The horse or pony should be trotted up in hand as slowly as possible. A pony lame in the foreleg will nod his head each time the sound leg comes to the ground. If lame behind, the weight will be seen to fall on the sound leg when it comes to the ground.

161. Laminitis is usually caused by excessive feeding, particularly with very lush grass, or by fast trotting on hard roads.

A lambswool pad beneath the girth will relieve pressure on girth galls

162. Colic is stomach ache in a horse. First give him a colic drink, and move him to a place of safety so that he cannot become cast in his stall or box if he tries — and he usually will — to get down and roll. He should be covered with a rug and walked slowly round. Serious cases must be dealt with quickly by a vet.

163. Colic is usually caused by irregularities in feeding, sudden changes in diet, bad hay, or by sand and other impurities in the drinking water, particularly when the horse has to water from a shallow river bed.

164. A horse or pony's normal temperature is 100.5°. A rise of one degree may not be important, but a temperature above 102° shows that something is really wrong.

165. With a cold in the head a yellow or white discharge can be seen from both nostrils. This can be quite profuse and even enough to soil a manger, the edges of a stable door or the ground.

166. Strangles is a contagious disease usually confined to young horses, but older animals can get it if they have never contracted it in their youth. The illness starts with a sharp rise in temperature, sometimes as high as 105°. There is usually profuse nasal catarrh and an abscess starts to form in the jowl region. The horse becomes greatly distressed. It can only swallow with difficulty and the throat region becomes large and intense with the result that the horse goes off his feed. In due course the abscess between the jaw bones bursts and drains, bringing immediate relief. The horse must be isolated and care must be taken to ensure that he has separate feeding and watering utensils.

167. Broken wind is a chronic and incurable disease of the lungs. It is characterised by a persistant cough, heaving flanks and distress when the horse moves, making it almost impossible to perform fast work, because of a double effort at expiration.

47

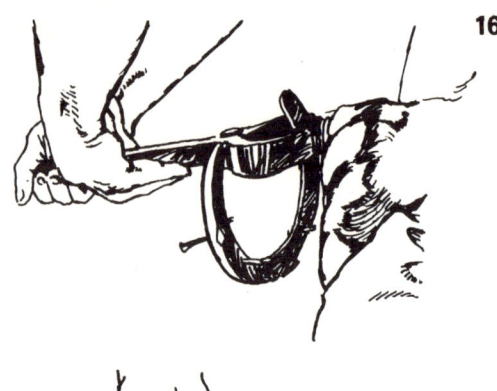

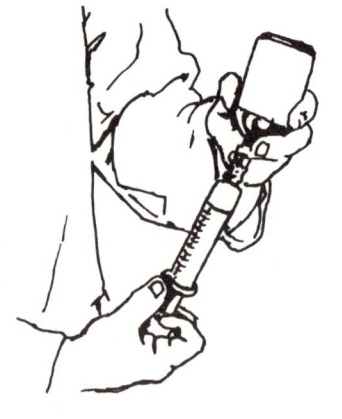

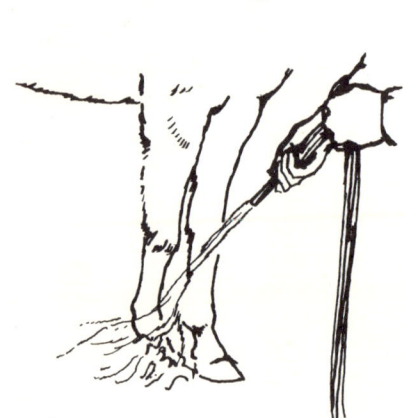

168. The four most common types of wounds are:
(1) Clean cut wounds, caused by a sharp object like a piece of metal or glass.

(2) Torn wounds when the skin or flesh has a tear caused by something like a nail or barbed wire.

(3) Punctured wounds which are caused by stakes, nails or even penetrating types of thorns. They are sometimes difficult to find because the entrance may be small although the penetration may be deep. They are always serious, particularly near a joint.

(4) Bruised wounds, caused by kicks, blows, galls, overreaches or falls.

Advanced Answers

169. Fine nailing occurs when the nail penetrates too little of the wall so that the shoe is insecure.

Coarse nailing occurs when the nail comes out too high up the wall of the foot.

170. Coarse nailing can be dangerous when a nail is driven in too high and may go too close to the sensitive structures of the foot causing 'nail binding' or 'pricked foot', either of which can cause lameness.

171. A feather-edged shoe is useful when a horse is inclined to 'brush' or hit and injure the opposite leg. The inner branch of the shoe is 'feathered' and fitted close in under the wall reducing the risk of striking the opposite leg. The inner branches of this type of shoe have fewer nail holes.

172. After finding out which leg is affected, you should look for heat, pain and swelling. All three may not necessarily be in evidence, and if the trouble is in the foot there will not be any swelling because the foot cannot expand. Because about 90% of the lameness is centred in the foot, the examination should begin there and work upwards. A constant comparison with the other leg will show any unusual swellings.

173. A pony with laminitis stands on the heels with the feet thrust forward, and can only be moved with difficulty. There is usually heat in the foot.

You would deal with the trouble by first calling a vet. The shoes should be removed and the feet cut down. The feed must be reduced to small bran mashes with Epsom salts added, and the pony will need cold applications applied to his feet. Use a hose pipe or stand the pony in a stream. An early injection of anti-histamine or a cortisone drug can sometimes bring remarkable relief. When improvement is shown the pony should be shod with a special surgical shoe and turned out to graze on poor land. If the land is not particularly poor, grazing time should be limited to about two hours daily.

174. He probably has colic.

175. A horse with a cold should be taken off work and isolated. He will need plenty of fresh air without draughts and should be rugged-up and bandaged. Feed him at ground level to allow the nostrils to drain and ensure he has a separate water bucket. Bran mashes are good. His nostrils need cleaning three times a day with cotton wool which should then be burnt. His head should be steamed and the vet sent for if his temperature goes above 102°.

176. The cough characterised in broken wind is short and dry and sometimes described as 'graveyard'. It appears to come from the region of the belly. With time and rest the cough may become less marked and less frequent.

177. Azoturia or 'Monday morning disease' is a sudden breakdown of fibres in the big muscles of the loins and quarters of a horse, and is associated with strong muscular exertion following a period of rest on a full working diet. The cause is really unknown but while at work the horse slackens pace and becomes stiff in his action.

Conditions can get worse so that he staggers and sways or even falls. Blow-

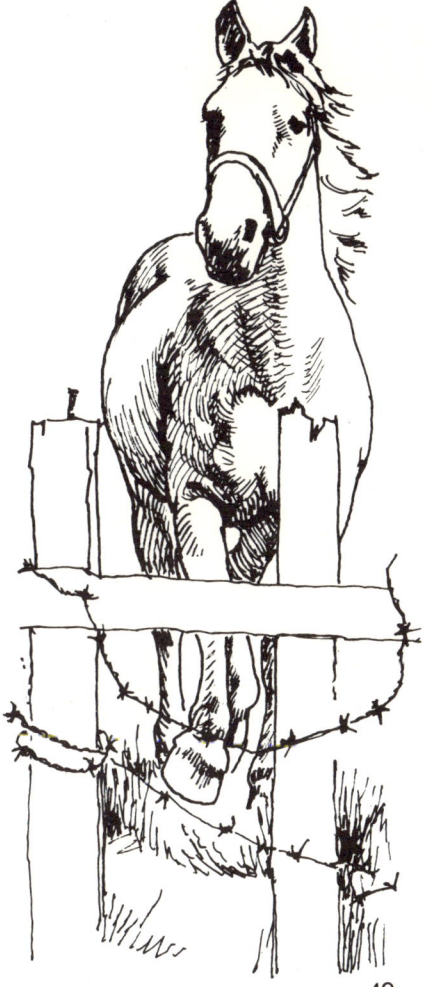

Artificial aids

ing and sweating can also take place, and the muscles of the quarters become hard and tense with muscular tremors. The rider should immediately dismount, slacken the girth, and throw a jacket or some other form of covering over the loins. The horse should be allowed to rest and then either be taken home by box or found shelter nearby. He should be rugged-up, kept warm and made comfortable. He will need plenty of drinking water, and a laxative diet. The affected muscles should be massaged and treated with hot packs, and an electric blanket can be very useful. If possible an electric fire should be rigged up overhead so that heat can play on the affected muscles. The horse will need rest for four or five days, as permanent damage can result if the illness is not treated properly. It is certainly as well to take veterinary advice as soon as possible.

178. Consumption in a horse is a disease of the belly or bones and not of the chest as in humans. It is more likely to be found in horses 15 years of age or older.

179. Lockjaw or tetanus is a serious disease caused by a germ which lives in the soil getting into the body by way of a wound. The disease develops after about ten days and stiffness of movement and shooting of the third eyelid across the eye is characteristic of the condition. Immediate treatment is essential. The main trouble can be prevented by an early dose of lockjaw serum whenever a horse gets a cut or a wound. Protection for life by injection of doses of tetanus toxoid is the best method.

180. To drench a horse, raise its head and administer the fluid slowly from a bottle. Allow one mouthful to be swallowed before another is given. A horse's head can be raised by fastening a head-rope to the middle-front of the noseband and passing the free end over a beam. His head must be lowered immediately he coughs.

Horsemanship

Novice Answers

181. It is important before mounting to make sure that the girths are tight and the stirrup irons are down.

182. When you throw a leg over the horse's withers the reins will have to be dropped and control of the horse lost. Any movement the horse makes can catch the rider off balance and cause a fall.

183. It is usual to mount and dismount on the nearside, but it is correct to mount and dismount on either side, and it is always as well to practise from either side in case of emergencies.

184. The seat just means the rider's position in the saddle and the security and control he has over the movements of the horse. A good seat depends upon a combination of balance, suppleness and grip.

185. To measure the correct length of a stirrup leather, stand facing the saddle, and place the knuckles of the fingers on the right hand on the stirrup bar of the saddle. The leather and iron should then reach into the arm pit.

186. The pace of the trot is two-time, the canter is three-time.

187. The little finger of each hand should divide the two reins with the bridoon rein held on the outside.

188. The word aid can either mean:
    (1) The way in which a rider signals his intentions, so that a horse can be taught to understand and obey them.
    (2) The means a rider has for producing those signals.

189. Natural aids are the hands, legs, body and voice. Artificial aids are such things as whips, spurs and martingales.

Walk

Trot

Canter

Gallop

190. The whip should be held in the palm of the hand and allowed to lie in front of the rider's legs.

191. To increase pace to a walk or a trot both legs should be closed, the back straightened and pressure on the reins eased while still maintaining light contact with the mouth. As soon as the horse obeys, only slight pressure of the legs is needed to maintain the necessary pace.

192. To decrease the pace close both legs, straighten the back and bring the horse up with the hands still. The pace of the horse should be reduced smoothly and the head carriage should be steady. At the halt he should stand squarely on all four legs. The pressure of the legs and reins should be relaxed as soon as the horse has obeyed the command.

Intermediate Answers

193. Dressage helps improve the standard of training of a horse used for riding. It is really a progressive system of movements to teach the horse to balance himself with the weight of his rider, without putting undue strain on joints or muscles, and so enable him to obey his rider's demands with the utmost grace and ease.

194. With shoulder-in the horse bends round the inside leg of the rider. The outside shoulder is in front of the inside hind quarter, while the inside legs pass in front of the outside legs. The horse's body is then said to be bent away from the direction in which he is travelling.

195. A horse is cantering true or united when the leading foreleg and the leading hind leg appear to be on the same side. He is said to be cantering disunited when the leading hind leg appears to be on the opposite side to the leading foreleg.

196. A horse may pull for a number of reasons. The most frequent are because he has a hard mouth, or because he is excited. He may also pull because he lacks balance and training or because the bit causes him pain and consequently fear. He could, of course, pull for a combination of these reasons.

197. It is wrong to use a more severe bit just because a horse pulls or becomes excited. It is much better to use a snaffle, and try and teach him how to relax his jaw.

198. When driving a horse at a gallop, the rider should sit well down in the saddle and push the horse on by means of his seat and legs. As soon as a horse responds and is galloping freely the rider should adopt a forward position with the weight of the body taken on the knees and stirrups. The weight should be off the saddle so that with the body forward the rider's weight rests naturally over the centre of gravity.

199. The hands check or allow the pace to be altered by way of contact with the horse's mouth and control of the forehand. The legs guide through impulsion, and they are also used to lead and control the hindquarters of the horse.

200. The voice can be used to assist in controlling the horse. It can check, frighten, encourage and soothe.

201. A horse approaching a jump lowers his head and stretches his neck to balance himself as he prepares to make his jump.

202. A horse taking off shortens his neck, raises his head slightly and lifts his fore hand. As he brings his hocks under him he stretches his head and neck, springing forward and upwards. The head and neck are stretched to the full extent in the air, and slightly downwards with the hind legs off the ground and gathered up under the belly. On landing his head comes up and his neck again shortens.

203. Jumping fences in a continuous straight line tends to excite a horse. Jumping fences in a circle will quieten a horse down and encourages him to be supple.

204. To find a horse's stiff side, the rider should walk the horse on a loose rein, and pick up the left or near rein. If the horse quickly responds by turning his head to the left, and goes in that direc-

Avoid jumping fences in a continuous straight line as this may tend to excite.

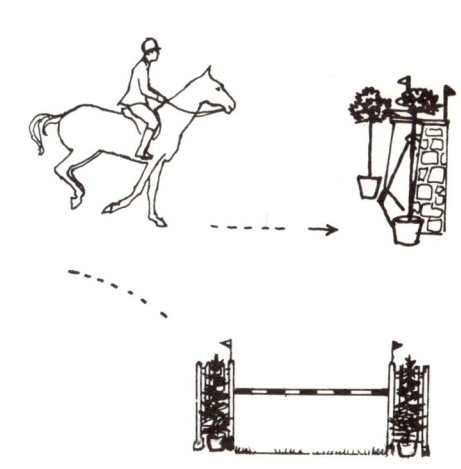

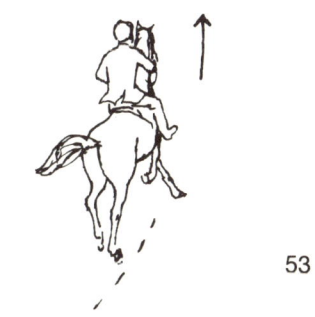

On the bit

Evading the pressure of the bit

tion, that is most likely to be the soft side.

When the rider drops the left rein and picks up the right rein and finds the horse is against turning his head to the right, but will only move in that direction with a stiff jaw and neck, and his head straight, then that will almost certainly be the hard side.

Advanced Answers

205. A horse can be said to be cantering false or counter-lead if he is cantering to the left with the off-fore leading.

206. A dry mouth occurs when a horse's tongue has been drawn back with the mouth slightly open. The air passes quickly through the mouth drying it up. In such a dry state the bars of the mouth easily be bruised or torn.

207. A horse usually swallows his tongue or puts it over the bit when he is trying to evade the pressure of the bit.

208. A half-pass is when a horse moves on two tracks with the head, neck and shoulders always slightly ahead of the quarters. This movement always looks much more graceful if there is a slight bend, so that the horse is looking in the direction of the movement. It also gives the outside shoulders more freedom. In this movement the outside legs pass and cross in front of the inside legs. The inside legs are the legs on the side to which a horse is bent and the opposite legs are consequently known as the outside legs.

209. In the turn of the forehand the horse's quarters move in regular steps round the inner foreleg. The position of the horse's head is important and the inner foreleg should act rather as a pivot and stay more or less on the same spot. The turn on the forehand should only be done from the halt.

210. The term rhythm in dressage is known as the ordered flow of movement, with regularity and evenness of the hoof beats.

211. For a horse to be on the bit, its hocks must be correctly placed, the neck raised and the head steady. The rider should have a light contact with the mouth and the horse should not offer any resistance to the rider's command.

212. When the rider's hands have no influence on the bit.

213. There are four steps to a stride at the walk.

There are two steps to a stride at the trot.

There are three steps to a stride at the canter.

There are four steps to a stride at the gallop.

214. If a horse develops a habit of rushing his fences, instead of schooling him over a line of fences, he should be ridden in a circle near a fairly simple type of fence. When he is going quietly the circle can be enlarged so that he can jump the fence. If he still plays up the circle should be made smaller and the fence missed out until he is quiet again.

215. When teaching a young horse to jump it is better to increase the spread rather than the height of a fence.

216. A horse will judge his distance from a jump by looking at the part of the fence on or nearest to the ground. It is consequently easier if he is given a distinct ground line like a pole.

Hunting

Hunting whip

Novice Answers

217. Cub hunting starts as soon as the corn is cut and usually ends during the last week of October or the first week in November.

218. Fox hunting officially ends on April 30th.

219. Puppy walkers are people who wish to help the Hunt by taking puppies and looking after them at home, from the time they are weaned, until they are ready to be taken into the kennels.

220. The titles of the Hunt staff are the Huntsman, the kennelman and the whippers-in. In small establishments there may be only one kennelman and one whipper-in. If the Master hunts hounds, there is usually a kennel-huntsman.

221. Correct hacking clothes with a hard hat as a protection against overhanging boughs is the correct dress for cub hunting. A hunting whip with a thong is very important.

222. A hunting whip and thong is necessary because you may need the thong to hold out beyond the hindquarters of your horse or pony to warn young hounds not to come too close. The whip should not be cracked on a hound.

223. This keeps a fox cub in the covert.

224. When a hound chases the wrong sort of quarry he is said to riot.

225. You may only get in front of hounds if the Huntsman asks you to help him stop hounds. This is usually when he is having trouble with his hounds hunting riot, or if they are in danger by going towards a railway line.

226. The shortened form of the word beware out hunting is 'ware' pronounced 'war'.

227. Hounds are counted in pairs known as couples.

228. This term is used to signal departure of a fox with a holloa.

Intermediate Answers

229. A hound enjoys the following food to keep him healthy: meat, oatmeal, hammered oatmeal, uveca or maize meal, potatoes, offal, hound biscuits, swedes or turnips, green vegetables, water cress, cod liver oil.

230. Cubbing meets are usually held at dawn or early in the morning, to take advantage of any morning dew before the sun gets too hot.

231. Red coats or whatever the hunt colour may be, worn with grey or black bowler hats or panama hats has been traditionally the correct dress for members of the Hunt staff on hound exercise.

232. They are given plenty of road work to help them get fit and then keep fit, and to harden their feet.

233. Always refer to the fox as him. A fox should never be referred to as she or it.

234. The Hunt button is a button which has a design monogram or lettering distinctive of a particular Hunt. Only the Master can give a subscriber the right to wear it.

235. 'Hounds please' is the warning given to the field to keep clear of hounds, and to get horses out of their way.

236. A hunting tie or stock is a specially shaped scarf of white linen or pique worn round the neck, the ends being passed through a loop at the back of the neck then brought round and knotted in the front where they should be held together with a plain solid safety pin.

237. The country is the territory hunted by a pack of hounds.

238. Hounds are said to be at fault when they check.

239. Hounds are said to run up together when they hunt closely together, and there are no stragglers.

240. Hounds are said to draw up wind when the Huntsman puts into a covert so that they must draw into or against the wind. When they draw in the same direction as the wind they are said to draw down wind.

Advanced Answers

241. A brass button is worn with a scarlet coat. A black bone button is worn with a black coat.

242. The Hunt Master wears the ribbons on the hunt cap pointing downwards.

243. A fadge is another name for a 'hound jog' which is usually about six miles an hour when travelling on the roads.

244. A bona fide hunter is a horse which has been regularly and fairly hunted and whose owner has been granted a hunters certificate by the Master of the pack concerned.

245. A hound hunt is one in which with very little scent the hounds continue to hunt their quarry by skill and perseverance.

246. If the whipper-in tells the Huntsman 'We want a couple' it means that there are two hounds missing.

247. A pack is said to be carrying a good head when they run well together with several leading hounds running level in front, as opposed to one hound leading.

248. A hound is said to be entered when he has hunted a fox.

249. A hound throws his tongue when he 'speaks' to the scent of a fox.

250. A babbler is a hound who continues to throw his tongue, or speaks long after the rest of the pack has hunted on.

251. A hound is said to have a toe down when a joint has been damaged so that the whole toe becomes straight and will not function.

252. A pack is all on when all the hounds brought out are present.

A huntsman

General Knowledge

Cleveland Bay

Novice Answers

253. An Australian cheeker is a racing device which is made of rubber, and lifts the bit in the horse's mouth. It is used to stop a horse from getting his tongue over the bit.

254. A horse shoe has seven nail holes, three on the inside and four on the outside.

255. The grakle noseband is named after the Grand National winner who wore one.

256. The Kimblewick bit was produced from a Spanish design for Mr. Phil Oliver, and named by him after the village where he lived.

257. Conformation is the term given to a horse's make and shape.

Palomino

258. A Palomino is not a breed of horse or pony but a colour type. Usually it is varying shades of gold with a chalk white mane and tail.

259. A draught horse is a horse used for drawing any vehicle. Typical examples are the Hackney, Cleveland Bay, etc.

260. A dragsman is a coachman.

261. A draw rein is a rein attached to the girth and passing to the hand through the rings of the bit.

262. A dutch slip is a simple form of head collar made of leather or tubular web, suitable for foals.

Hackney

263. Flecked is where small collections of white hairs occur distributed irregularly in any part of a horse's coat.

264. A filly is a female horse under the age of four.

Intermediate Answers

265. A log is a solid block of wood with a hole in the centre. A rope is passed through

Dutch Slip

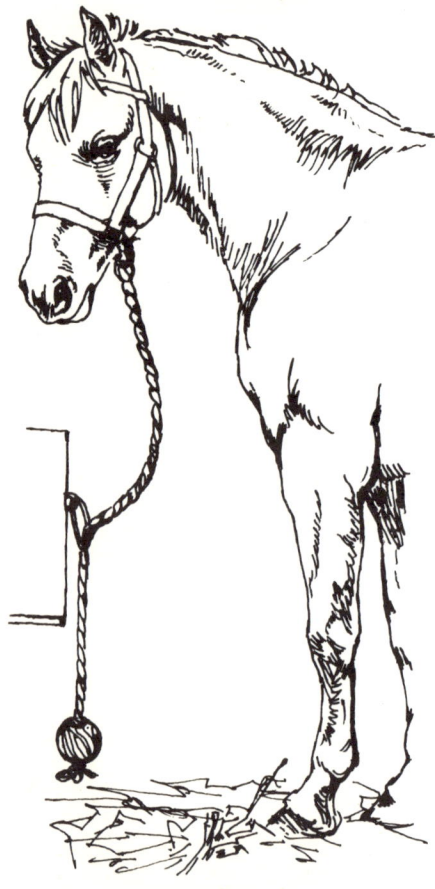

The use of the log allows a horse limited head movement

the hole and knotted, and the other end is passed through a manger ring allowing a horse limited head movement.

266. The recommended size for a loose box is 10 x 12 feet x 10 feet in height.

267. The best time for a mare to foal is about the first week in April because there are not many flies about, and the foal is able to spend much of its time lying down peacefully in the field. The grass is also growing to its best then, and will increase the mare's milk at a time when she needs it most.

268. Flagging is another term for docking.

269. Runners are leather loops on saddlery, especially the bridle, that slide up and down to allow the strap ends to pass through.

270. Horse-sick is the term applied to pastures which have become soured by horses grazing them for too long.

271. A Horse Standard is the correct name for a measuring stick.

272. A garter is a narrow leather strap and buckle on hunting or riding boots, which passes through a loop at the rear of the boot, and in the front is buckled between the second and third button of the breeches.

273. The seat of corn is the terminal position of the wings of the sole between the bars and the wall at the heel.

274. A Connemara is a pony breed originating in Western Eire. It shows signs of Spanish and Arab blood and is predominantly grey in colour. It is hardy, docile and intelligent, and usually stands between 13 - 14 hands high.

275. A brougham is probably the most popular type of closed carriage for one or two horses.

276. False ribs are to the rear of the eighth rib.

There are eight true and ten false ribs.

Advanced Answers

277. The first hunting monarch in England was King Penda of Mercia (577 - 655). It is always said that his huntsman lived near Pytchley Village.

278. A hybrid is a cross between a horse on the one side and an ass or zebra on the other side.

279. Lonsdale girth straps are straps which extend beneath the saddle flap, and are used with a special short girth. The system removes most of the girth buckles from under the thigh, and is used frequently on dressage saddles.

280. A loriner is a manufacturer of bits, spurs, stirrups etc.

281. A troika is a Russian term for a team of three horses driven abreast usually before an open carriage.

282. A wagon-lock is a type of iron shoe which is placed under the rear wheel of a cart to help prevent it going too fast downhill.

283. A garron is a general name for the ponies of Scotland and Ireland.

284. The mark is the dark centre of the tooth of a young horse, and is used to help tell the age of a horse.

285. A jaunting car is a two wheel Irish horse drawn vehicle in which the passengers sit facing the sides of the road with the feet on platforms which fold up.

286. A jarde or jardon is a callous tumour found on the outside of a horse's hock.

287. A ewe-necked horse is one where the crest of the neck, between the poll and the withers, is concave rather than convex.

288. Beans can also refer to the black centres of a horse's or pony's incisor teeth.

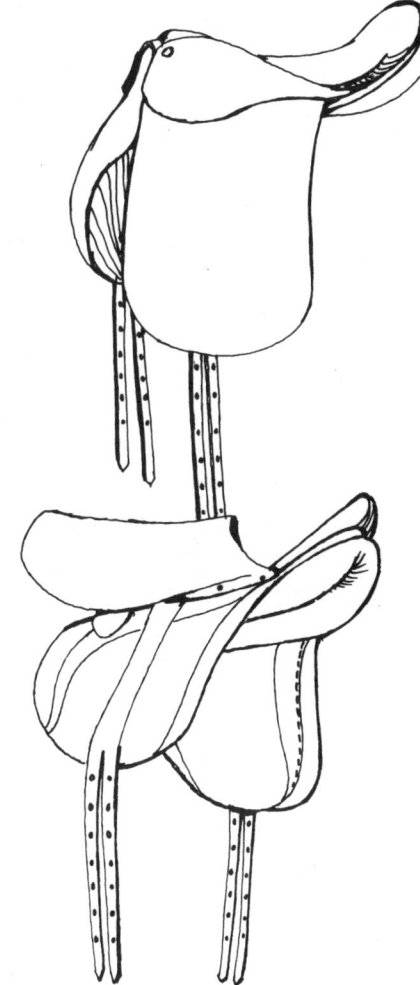

Dressage saddle with Lonsdale girths

Ewe-necked horse